ISBN 978-0-265-06052-0
PIBN 10952956

Historic, archived document

Do not assume content reflects current
scientific knowledge, policies, or practices.

ISSUED WEEKLY BY
THE FOREIGN AGRICULTURAL SERVICE
BUREAU OF AGRICULTURAL ECONOMICS
UNITED STATES DEPARTMENT OF AGRICULTURE
WASHINGTON, D.C.

Vol. 28   MARCH 12, 1934   No. 11

FEATURE ARTICLES

UNITED STATES AGRICULTURAL EXPORTS

MANCHURIAN SOY BEAN SITUATION

- - - - - - - - - -

IN THIS ISSUE

	Page
LATE CABLES	276
Germany extends grain export certificate system	277
Peru plans to increase wheat production	278
Chile to control wheat trade and fix prices	280
World cotton consumption largest in four years	281
Japan maintains cotton yarn production	282
Australia and New Zealand expect large apple crops	283
Canadian peach buds frozen	284
World production of hops increased	284
United States agricultural exports again low	284

L A T E   C A B L E S

- - - - -

London wool sales opened March 6, with prices for all
types from 5 to 15 percent lower than at close of January
sales. Super merinos and fine crossbreds nearest steady.
On March 9, sales were slow and catalogues reduced, some
owners preferring to withhold. Greatest weakness in
greasy 40's and 50's. Yorkshire and Germany the chief
buyers. (Agricultural Attache Edward Foley, London,
March 6 and 9, 1934.)

CROP AND MARKET PROSPECTS

BREAD GRAINS

Germany extends export certificate system

German export certificates provided for wheat exports from March 8 to July 15, 1934 will permit the duty free importations of barley and corn and also, to a certain extent, of oilcake, according to cabled advices from the Berlin office of the Foreign Agricultural Service. Under the grain exchange plan for this crop year as during the past 2 years, wheat exported was given an export certificate which entitled the holder to reimport a like quantity of wheat at any time during the entire season. A stimulus for early exports was provided by allowing free imports for certificates issued prior to December 1, 1933 (date extended to January 1, 1934) while in the case of certificates for later imports a customs rate of 7.5 marks per metric ton (8.09 cents per bushel at current exchange) was scheduled.

Imports of wheat have been very steady so far this year though on a lower level than in previous years, the Bureau's Berlin representatives point out. Exports of German wheat from August through December 1933, on the other hand, not only exceeded previous years but the export surplus will permit the duty free importation of about 1,100,000 bushels of wheat a month during the remainder of the present crop seasons regardless of future exports. See following table. This excess along with the duty on reimports and a decline in the sale price of the certificates with their consequent retarding effect on exports, also the shortage of feed grain supplies appears to be the principle reasons for extending the export certificates to the feed grains and products.

GERMANY: Imports and exports of wheat and flour, in terms of grain, August-September 1931-1933

Month	Imports			Exports		
	1931	1932	1933	1931	1932	1933
	1,000 bushels	1,000 bushels	1,000 bushels	1,000 bushels	1,000 bushels	1,000 bushels
August	1,801	3,638	2,278	74	1,470	1,948
September	2,535	2,719	2,205	3,086	5,107	3,968
October	2,425	3,013	2,719	2,793	4,530	3,858
November	2,499	2,499	2,682	2,682	3,333	4,813
December	3,380	2,939	2,388	2,315	2,168	4,446
Total	12,640	14,808	12,272	10,950	16,608	19,033

Berlin Office, Foreign Agricultural Service.

CROP AND MARKET PROSPECTS, CONT'D

- - - - - - - -

Barley and corn imports have been possible to a limited extent this season on the exchange basis for rye export certificates and also for oats certificates, though the latter method requires the payment of some duty. Certificates on rye exports effected before December 1 entitled the holder to free reimports while oats export certificates issued to that time permitted for the reimport of barley and corn at a customs charge of 2 marks per 100 kilos (36 cents per 100 pounds). This rate is an attempt to equalize the differences in the relative price levels of these feed grains. In the case of later exports of rye, reimports of barley and corn are subject to a customs rate of .50 marks per 100 kilos and for imports in exchange for oats exports, a customs rate of 2.50 marks per 100 kilos (9 and 45 cents per 100 pounds respectively). These regulations for wheat, rye and oats also refer to their respective milling products as well as the grains.

In addition to the free imports of barley and corn for the wheat export certificates importers using these certificates will receive 25 marks per metric ton (about 45 cents per 100 pounds at current exchange) in the form of negotiable paper which is acceptable only in payments on the monopoly charge for foreign oilcake. This procedure, as in the case of the exchange value of oats export certificates, helps to equalize the exchange value of the export certificates for different products.

Peru plans to increase wheat production

Wheat production in Peru is expected to increase in the near future, according to a report from Vice Consul J. Kenly Bacon at Callao-Lima. The Peruvian government and the Peruvian Corporation which operates most of the railroads of the country are now encouraging the farmers to grow more wheat by offering special inducements for the planting, harvesting, and marketing of this crop.

Although wheat has been grown to some extent in Peru since the time of the Spanish conquest, it has only been within the past few years that an organized effort has been made to develop its cultivation and increase acreage and production. The extensive communal pampas of the mountainous regions, about 10,000 feet above the level of the sea, are said to be good for the growing of wheat. Two reasons are cited to explain why it has not been profitably grown in the past: First, the high cost of transporting the grain from the pampas to the coast; second, the difficulty in teaching the communal Indian landowners the use of modern agricultural methods.

The company operating the Central Railroad of Peru has made an agreement with the Peruvian government to be in force for a year, whereby the Central Railroad will transport all wheat, seed, fertilizer, and agricultural machinery free of charge and will also plant and cultivate wheat on the communal lands in the Departments of Junin and Huancavelica. The government is to furnish the

CROP AND MARKET PROSPECTS, CONT'D

- - - - - -

seed and 100 tons of guano for fertilizer. The Indians who own the lands
will only be required to prepare and work the land on which the wheat is to be
planted. Since the railroad will also market the grain in Lima and Callao,
the Indians should be greatly benefited by this agreement.

The government of Peru is planning to purchase and distribute some 500
tons of "Marquis" seed, which with another imported variety called "Kanred",
has been the most successful imported wheat seed planted in Peru. It is hoped
that the farmers will produce enough wheat to supply domestic needs and there-
by reduce imports of wheat from abroad.

In 1932 there were 292,000 acres planted to wheat, and 3,117,000 bushels
of wheat were harvested, the average yield per acre being 10.7. The smaller
yield was the result of crop damage and disease that season. The best years
recorded since 1920 were 1929 and 1930, when 4,453,000 and 4,525,000 bushels
of wheat were produced from 351,000 and 353,000 acres respectively, with an
average yield of almost 13 bushels. No estimates for 1933 acreage or production have been received yet. See acreage and production table below.

Since Peru has not in the past produced sufficient wheat to meet domestic
needs, large quantities of both wheat and wheat flour have been imported. In
1913 total imports of wheat and wheat flour, in terms of wheat, amounted to
2,000,000 bushels; in 1929 and 1931 more than 4,000,000 bushels were shipped into
the country. In other years the totals have varied between these two amounts.
Imports from the United States have fallen off in recent years. In 1928, about
30 percent of Peru's wheat imports came from the United States and practically
all of the flour imports. In 1932, only 2,000 bushels of wheat were supplied by
the United States and flour had fallen to less than half of the amount furnished
in 1931, but total imports also declined sharply.. See import tables, page 302.

PERU: Acreage, production, and yield per acre, of wheat,
average 1920-24, 1925-29, annual 1926-1932

Year	Acreage	Production	Yield per acre
	Acres	Bushels	Bushels
Average 1920-24	240,000	2,802,000	11.7
Average 1924-29	268,000	3,307,000	12.3
1926	218,000	2,673,000	12.3
1927	284,000	3,149,000	11.1
1928	259,000	3,075,000	11.9
1929	351,000	4,453,000	12.7
1930	353,000	4,525,000	12.8
1931	288,000	3,485,000	12.1
1932....................	292,000	3,117,000	10.7

Statistical Abstract of Peru, Boletin de la Direccion Nacional de Estadistica,
and Report of Vice Consul J. Kenly Bacon.

CROP AND MARKET PROSPECTS, CONT'D

- - - - - - - -

Chile to control wheat trade and fix prices

In view of an expected increase in the 1934 wheat harvest and in order to protect the wheat farmers, a law was passed by the Government of Chile on February 1, 1934, authorizing the Chilean Agricultural Export Board to purchase wheat and wheat products for export whenever it is determined that there will be a surplus above home requirements. The price to be paid was fixed at 60 pesos per quintal ($1.64 per bushel at current rate of exchange) and to prevent speculation by brokers or middlemen, no purchases may be made except from producers or agricultural entities of the country. On the other hand, states a report from Consul Atwood at Santiago, should there be a shortage of wheat in Chile, the Board is to import wheat from abroad, duty free, and to resell it in Chile at such prices as will cover the cost of such transactions. This law will be in force until June 30, 1935.

When it is known that there will be a surplus of wheat, the President of Chile has the authority to fix the maximum amount available for export during a given period not to exceed one year. He may arrange for internal renewable credits for as much as 40,000,000 Chilean pesos (about $4,000,000 at current rate of exchange) for use by the Export Board in executing the new law.

Other interesting features of the law as cited by the Consul are: (1) The modification of the Chilean Customs Tariff, whereby wheat arriving abroad ship in a Chilean port valued at 70 pesos or more per quintal ($1.91 per bushel) may be admitted free of duty, while 1 gold pesos shall be charged for each peso if valued lower than 70 pesos per quintal. (2) If wheat is purchased in Chile at a price lower than that fixed by the Agricultural Export Board, a fine is to be collected amounting to 20 pesos per quintal (55 cents per bu.), which may be doubled in case of reconvictions, and the revenue thus derived will be credited to the Board and applied to administrative costs. (3) The maximum price of ordinary bread is placed at 1.40 pesos per kilo (6.4 cents per pound) and the cheapest quality is to be sold at 1.30 pesos per kilo (5.9 cents per pound).

In fixing the price to be paid for wheat by the Board, slight variations from the 60 pesos per quintal ($1.64 a bushel) will be permitted due to differences in freight and handling charges, but deliveries of wheat to Providencia Station, Santiago, and Ovalle (leading city in the northern most wheat growing region of Chile) must bring the price stated. At Talcahuano (chief port of south central Chile) a price of 54.50 pesos is stipulated and at Valchvia (leading city of southern Chile) 53 pesos per quintal. These prices are to be applied to wheat that is clean, healthy, dry and weighing at least 78 kilograms per hectoliter (60.5 lbs. per bushel). Warehousemen are allowed to purchase direct from producer at a reduction of 1.20 pesos per quintal (3.3 cents per bushel) in order to protect small growers from the high commissions sometimes charged by intermediaries and to assure them of a prompt disposal of their crop on known conditions. For a statement on the wheat industry of Chile, see "Foreign Crops and Markets", October 16, 1934.

CROP AND MARKET PROSPECTS, CONT'D

COTTON

World cotton consumption largest for four years

During the six months ended January 31, 1934 the total world mill consumption of all cotton increased 637,000 running bales or 5 percent over the corresponding months of the previous season, amounting to 12,519,000 bales, according to data just received by the Bureau of Agricultural Economics from the International Federation. This was the largest consumption for any half year period since the first half of 1929-30, when the world consumption of all cotton amounted to 13,202,000 bales. The 7,018,000 bales of American cotton consumed was 302,000 bales less than during the last half of the 1932-33 season, but the largest for any corresponding period since 1929-30. The smaller consumption of American during the last six months than in the preceding half year is accounted for by the smaller consumption in the United States. The decline in the United States consumption was due to the fact that during the latter part of the 1932-33 season domestic consumption, stimulated by speculative demand growing out of the currency situation, probable increased manufacturing costs under the N. R. A; , and improving conditions, reached the highest levels in the history of the domestic industry.

World consumption of "sundries" cotton (cotton other than American, Indian, and Egyptian) during the six months ended January 31 amounted to 2,607,000 running bales. This was about 100,000 bales larger than either of the two previous six month periods and was the largest since the first half of 1929-30. While consumption by countries has not been received, the increase in the consumption of this cotton was apparently accounted for by the larger consumption of domestically produced cotton in China and Russia, the two principal cottons included in "sundries". The consumption of Indian cotton was reported at 2,355,000 bales, the largest for any six month period since the first half of 1931-32. With the supply of Indian cotton for this season the largest since 1930-31, and increased mill activity in most parts of the world and with the smaller supply of American cotton it is natural that consumption of Indian should increase.

The 541,000 running bales (approximately 750 pounds) of Egyptian cotton reported by the Federation as having been consumed during the first half of the season represented an increase of 14 percent over the preceding six month period and 17 percent over the corresponding period last season. Although the supply of Egyptian cotton has in several seasons been larger than in the present season, the reported world consumption in the first half of this season was larger than in any half year period since comparable reports were begun in 1920-21. This development is at least partly explained by the fact that cotton mill activity has been greater than in some of the other years, the more favorable price parity between Egyptian and American than in some of the earlier years, and perhaps in part to the change which has occurred in the Egyptian Government's cotton policy. During the past year or more the Egyptian Government has, instead

- - - - - - -

of buying cotton and holding it off the market, been making special efforts
to encourage foreign countries to take more Egyptian cotton.

Mill stocks of all kinds of cotton on February 1 were reported at
5,216,000 bales compared with 4,542,000 bales a year earlier and were the
second largest for the period since records became available. All four of
the groups reported by the Federation showed substantial increases over the
last few years, due perhaps in some cases to the larger supplies as well as
the higher rate of mill consumption, and possibly to some speculative accumulation of stocks. The 2,833,000 bales of American cotton held by mills on
February 1 represented the largest figure for that date since 1929, and the
1,203,000 running bales of Indian the largest since 1931. Stocks of Egyptian
were reported at 242,000 bales and other growths "sundries" at 938,000 bales,
both of which were equal to or larger than in any year since records became
available in 1921.

Cotton yarn production in Japan well maintained

Imports of American cotton in Japan during the month of January were
slightly higher than in December and reached the large amount of 236,168
bales of 500 pounds according to a report received from Vice Consul Walter
P. McConaughy at Kobe, Japan. Other developments during January were: A
slight decline in yarn production compared with the two preceding record break-
ing months, decreased production and exports of piece goods and slightly larger
stocks of raw cotton. There were no imports of Indian cotton but following the
Japanese-Indian agreement shipments were in transit to Japan.

Spot prices of cotton were up 10 percent during the month at Osaka
following New York and Liverpool advances and a heavy volume of future transactions was recorded. Imminent resumption of Indian cotton imports stimulated
transactions in Indian cotton. The average price difference between Indian
Oomra-Akola and American Strict Middling was about 22 percent. Mill takings
of American cotton were smaller than in preceding months due to slightly
decreased yarn production and heavy mill holdings of American cotton. Mill
takings were 160,000 bales of American, 12,000 bales Indian, 13,000 bales
Egyptian and 19,000 bales others. Stocks of cotton on January 31 were considered
abnormally large although not equal to stocks of a year ago. Stocks of
American cotton in port warehouses and sheds were 425,000 bales. Yarn production of 270,728 bales in January compares with a production of 281,000 bales in
December and 280,800 bales in November.

January yarn production represents a slight decline from the previous
two months but there is no prospect of a continued decline in yarn production,
according to the Vice Consul. A recent agreement among members of the Japan
Cotton Spinners Association to reduce curtailment percentages from 27.6 to 22.6
percent for the third quarter of 1934 indicates a probability of additional
production. New spindles are continually being added to the Japanese industry

CROP AND MARKET PROSPECTS, CONT'D

- - - - - - -

and enlarging the productive capacity. Spinners are confident of an adequate demand from weavers although yarn stocks are gradually increasing.

Exports of cotton cloth in January were 155,000,000 square yards compared to 186,000,000 yards in December. Exportations to India under the newly inaugurated quotas are proceeding smoothly. Negotiations are in progress between Japan and Great Britain and between Japan and the Netherlands relating to the textile trade of Japan with the Oriental dependencies of Great Britain and the Netherlands respectively.

- - - - - - -

FRUIT, VEGETABLES AND NUTS

Australia and New Zealand expect large apple crops

Another large apple crop is in prospect for Australia and New Zealand. Exports to Europe are expected to be held to 6,000,000 boxes, which compares with the 6,752,000 shipped in the record but disastrous 1933 season, according to information issued by the British Empire Marketing Board. First shipments will land in March. On the 9th a small consignment of pears from Victoria is expected. Some apples from Australia are booked to land March 15. The first New Zealand fruit (probably some apples included) is expected to arrive March 30.

Judging by the disastrous prices received last season, quantities should probably have been restricted to considerably less than 6,000,000 boxes. The trade is of the opinion that 4,000,000 are all the British market can absorb at satisfactory prices which would leave 1,000,000 boxes to be shipped to the Continent, out of a total movement of 5,000,000 boxes. On the other hand the outlook for the Australian exports is better this season than last because there will be less competition from oranges during the summer and it is not likely that the English apple crop will develop prematurely this season as it did last.

Certain sizes (large and very small) and odd varieties will not be permitted to clear for export to Europe this year. The lowest grade (Plain) will also be kept out of export. The lack of uniform grading and packing, and the galaxy of varieties of apples grown, has been a drawback for several years to Australian growers. Tasmania is said to be the worst offender in this regard. The New Zealand pack is good.

The 4,807,000 boxes to go forward from Australia are composed of 2,750,000 from Tasmania, 780,000 from Victoria, 600,000 from Western Australia, 520,000 from South Australia, 120,000 from New South Wales, and 37,000 boxes from Queensland.

CROP AND MARKET PROSPECTS, CONT'D

- - - - - - - -

Canadian peach buds frozen

The peach crop in the Niagara Peninsula of Canada was severely damaged by the extremely cold weather during February, according to Vice-Consul Elton M. Hoyt at Niagara Falls, Ontario. Official reports from 3 of Canada's most important peach district indicate damage varying from light to almost total crop failure. In some previous years the United States has marked considerable quantities of peaches in Canada, especially before the duty was raised in August, 1930. During recent years Canadian peach production plus the fresh peach importations from the United States have been around 1,000,000 bushels. Production in the United States during the past two seasons has been approximately 45,000,000 bushels. See table, page 299, for exports of American peaches to Canada and figures on production in both countries.

- - - - - - - - - -

HOPS

Increase in world production of hops

The 1933 production of hops in the principal hop growing countries of Europe and in the United States is estimated at 93,933,000 pounds as compared with 75,867,000 pounds produced by these countries in 1932. The 1933 world hop crop, exclusive of Russia, but including rough estimates for production in countries for which statistics have not as yet been received, is estimated at 104,000,000 pounds which is 21 percent increase over the 1932 crop.

The world hop acreage for 1933 increased about 17 percent over 1932. The country showing the largest improvement in production over the 1932 crop is the United States, having produced 36,440,000 pounds, an increase of about 51 percent and the largest yield since 1916. See table page 304.

- - - - - - - - - -

UNITED STATES AGRICULTURAL EXPORTS AGAIN LOW

Expressed as an index number, United States exports of agricultural products for the month of January, 1934 stood at 93, the second lowest January index during the last 20 years. For all commodities except cotton the index was 72, a new low record for January. With the exception of fruits and dairy products, all groups shared in the decline.

Cotton exports dropped off when compared with January of 1932 and 1933. During the seven months ended January 31, the United States exported 5,929,000 bales valued at $296,786,000 as against 5,808,000 bales valued at $212,060,000 during the corresponding period of 1932-33, a gain of 2 percent in volume but

UNITED STATES AGRICULTURAL EXPORTS AGAIN LOW, CONT'D

an increase of 40 percent in value. The average export value rose from 7.3 cents per pound to 10.0 per pound in 1933-34. Exports of wheat and flour continued small though recording a gain over January a year ago. During the seven months period July 1933-January 1934, United States exports of wheat including flour amounted to 18,608,000 bushels valued at $13,797,000 as compared with 31,950,000 bushels valued at $19,261,000 during the same period of 1932-33, a decrease of 42 percent in quantity and 28 percent in value. Exports to Brazil and Greece which last season were our most important outlets dropped off sharply but exports to China rose to 4,340,000 bushels as compared with 546,000 bushels during the corresponding seven months of 1932-33.

The index for tobacco fell to 82, a decline when compared with the four preceding months and also with January a year ago. During the 7 months ended January 31 of the present year, 286,715,000 pounds of leaf tobacco valued at $63,733,000 were marketed abroad as compared with 246,049,000 pounds valued at $42,745,000 during the corresponding period a year ago, a gain of 17 percent in volume and 49 percent in value. The export position of fruit was better this month than last and was also above that for January 1932 and 1933. A better demand for fresh apples on the part of Germany, France, the Netherlands and the United Kingdom account for this increase. The index for cured pork was 17, one of the lowest monthly indexes on record and the volume of lard sent to foreign markets was smaller than for any January since 1920.

UNITED STATES: Index numbers of the volume of agricultural exports, January 1932, 1933, and 1934, as compared with previous months a/

Commodity	1932	1933			1934
	January	January	November	December	January
All commodities	111	97	111	109	93
All commodities, except cotton	81	73	79	93	72
Grain and products.........	74	38	33	63	45
Animal products............	75	92	72	73	68
Dairy products and eggs....	139	77	53	74	91
Fruit......................	329	267	432	329	346
Cotton fiber, incl. linters	134	116	135	120	109
Wheat, including flour.....	91	37	22	76	51
Tobacco, unmanufactured....	77	87	135	191	82
Hams and bacon.............	20	23	36	23	17
Lard	152	198	121	139	130

Foreign Agricultural Service. Compiled from official records of the Bureau of Foreign and Domestic Commerce. a/ July 1909-June 1914 = 100. For detailed figures on exports, see page

PROPOSED SCHEME FOR SUGAR MARKET CONTROL IN GREAT BRITAIN

In October 1934 the British Sugar (Subsidy) Act of 1925 expires. With its expiration, a subsidy which has been accorded to the domestic sugar industry over a period of 10 years will terminate unless legal provision is made for its continuation. As an alternative, assistance of another sort, not involving any payment by the government, may be secured by the domestic sugar industry under the provisions of the Agricultural Marketing Act of 1931. A Draft Scheme for taking advantage of the provisions of the Act was submitted to the Minister of Agriculture and Fisheries on February 1, 1934.

Under the old Sugar Act of 1925 a substantial subsidy was paid on raw sugar to manufacturers on the condition that they would pay a fixed minimum price to the grower of the beets. Through the impetus of the large grants obtained, both the agricultural phase and the precessing phase of the sugar industry showed a very rapid growth. In 1924-25, 22,400 acres were devoted to sugar beets, there were but three factories, and these produced about 50,000 long tons of sugar. In 1932-33 the acreage was 255,000, there were 16 factories, and these produced 659,000 long tons of sugat. Where it had supplied about 5 per cent of domestic requirements, the industry now furnished about 20 to 25 per cent.

But payment of the subsidy involved a heavy cost to the tax-payers. At the end of 1933 the Secretary of the Treasury reported that the total assistance given to the sugar industry up to that date (including aid extended as early as 1922) amounted to £37,442,000 (about $182,200,000 at par).

The Draft Scheme which is proposed to supplant the Sugar Act of 1925 differs from it in almost every important respect. In part, this difference follows from the nature of the Agricultural Marketing Act of 1931, as amended in 1933, which provides for statutory monopolies of the domestic market on the part of the domestic producers of any agricultural commodity when by a vote they indicate their desire for such a control. Whereas the old act did not concern itself with quantitative control, the proposed new plan is almost entirely a quota allotment scheme, with control vested in the domestic manufacturers and refiners of Great Britain. Moreover, when the old act specifically mentioned the grower and a minimum price for beets, the proposed Scheme makes no reference to him. It is concerned solely with the domestic manufacturers and refiners of Great Britain, and in its language limits the use of the term, producers, to them alone.

The Draft Scheme provides for the immediate creation of a Sugar Marketing Board and lists the names of 22 representatives, 11 of the sugar manufacturers and 11 of the sugar refiners, to constitute the first Board. The Board is to prepare a register of the sugar manufacturers and refiners whose processing operations are limited to Great Britain. Applicants for registration who manufacture sugar from beets grown in Great Britain are registered as manufacturers whether or not they also engage in refining, and all other domestic processors are classified as refiners.

PROPOSED SCHEME FOR SUGAR MARKET CONTROL IN GREAT BRITAIN, CONT'D

On the coming into force of this scheme, a poll of the registered producers is to be taken on the question whether the scheme is to remain in force. If the vote is favorable to the scheme, it is to come into force one month after-the declaration of the poll. Following that date, a manufacturer or refiner who is neither registered nor exempt from registration may not sell any sugar either in Great Britain or elsewhere. A registrant may not sell any refined sugar (either in Great Britain or elsewhere) during any quota period unless a quota has been determined for his case. If a quota has been determined he can not sell any quantity of refined sugar in excess of the quota and he can not sell any refined sugar (either in Great Britain or elsewhere) otherwise than under a contract specifying that the buyer shall permit the producer not to make delivery if such delivery involves exceeding of the quota. An excess margin of 1/20th of the quota is permitted to any registrant in any one year but any such excess must be offset by a reduction in his quota for the duration of the next year.

Quotas are to be determined by the Board not later than one month before the beginning of each sugar year, which comes on the Sunday nearest the first day of October. The quota of each registered producer is to be determined by reference to his qualifying tonnage. The latter figure consists of the number of tons of sugar sold during the 3-year period, January 1930 to December 1932. Quotas may be transferred by means of joint application to the Secretary of the Board on the part of the two registered producers involved.

It is noteworthy that voting power on the Board is distributed evenly between the processors of home grown beets and the processors of imported raw sugar instead of in the proportion of 1 to 3, which represents approximately the ratio of their respective contributions to the domestic supply. After the end of January 1935 the Board is to consist of 24 persons annually elected, 11 by the registered manufacturers, 11 by the refiners, and 2 by the elected Board members themselves. The same balance of power is observed in an Executive Committee of 7 appointed by the Board. Of this Committee 3 are to represent the manufacturers, 3 are to represent the refiners and 1 t, is to be chosen either by the Minister of Agriculture or by the Board itself.

Each year an election of members of the Board is to be held. Unless the number of candidates does not exceed the number of persons to be elected, a formal election is held, in which each registered producer receives a "standard number of votes", consisting of at least one vote plus an additional vote for every 10,000 tons comprised in his qualifying tonnage.

- - - - - - -

288

Foreign Crops and Markets

Col. 28, No. 11

MANCHURIAN SOYBEAN OUTPUT LARGER THAN LAST YEAR

The 1933 Manchurian soy bean crop is considered equal to the large 1931 crop and about 18 percent larger than the 1932 harvest, according to a report recently received from Fred J. Rossiter, Assistant Agricultural Commissioner at Shanghai, China. The Economic Research Committee of the South Manchurian Railway estimated this year's soy bean production at 5,736,000 short tons. The acreage was slightly larger than last year but somewhat smaller than in 1931. Weather conditions were favorable for the bean crop this past season resulting in a heavy yield per acre which was estimated by the South Manchurian Railway at 19 1/2 bushels per acre compared with an estimate of 16 1/2 bushels last year. The soy bean acreage in Manchuria in 1934 is not expected to be as large as in 1933. Low prices for beans may influence farmers to shift to other crops and propaganda to increase wheat and cotton acreage may slightly affect soy bean plantings this spring.

The total quantity of soy beans and bean products available for export during the current crop year (Oct. 1, 1933 to Sept. 30, 1934) is about 4,700,000 short tons. About 1,000,000 short tons is considered the average amount of beans used for home consumption and seed in Manchuria. With only 3,620,000 short tons as the total quantity exported during the past crop year, the disposal of the entire crop this season is considered a serious problem.

The carryover on September 30 from the 1932 bean crop was the smallest in several years, being estimated at 100,000 short tons, which compares with 200,000 tons the previous year. The total supply of beans in Manchuria for the 1933-34 crop year is therefore 5,836,000 short tons.

MANCHURIA: Estimated soy bean acreage and production, 1927 to 1933

Year	Area	Production
	Acres	Short tons
1927................	----	4,899,560
1928................	9,224,900	5,334,100
1929................	9,489,700	5,351,140
1930................	10,029,500	5,838,197
1931................	10,416,800	5,760,165
1932................	9,580,176	4,703,215
1933................	9,846,600	5,736,000

South Manchuria Railway.

The market demand for the 1933 soy beans is not expected to be much larger than last year, and with an extra million short tons available for export, the outlook for the disposal of this season's crop is not very encouraging. The present poor demand in Europe for soy beans must improve in order to prevent a large carryover on September 30, 1934. The demand for beans depends primarily upon the European market. Germany has issued regulations in respect to the amount of soy beans that may be imported but the extent if any, which these regulations will reduce imports is not known. With lower

MANCHURIAN SOYBEAN OUTPUT LARGER THAN LAST YEAR, CONT'D

prices some of the other European countries may use larger quantities. If
the German regulations do not reduce last year's imports, European imports
may be expected to exceed the past year's amount.

MANCHURIA: Soy bean production and distribution, 1929-30 to 1933-34

Crop year	Production	Carryover from last crop year	Total supply	Total exports	Carryover end of crop year	Home consumption and seed
	1,000 short tons	1,000 short tons	1,000 short tons	1,000 short tons	1,000 short tons	1,000 short tons
1929-30..........	5,351	250	5,601	4,414	200	987
1930-31..........	5,838	200	6,038	4,569	350	1,119
1931-32..........	5,760	350	6,110	4,717	200	1,093
1932-33..........	4,703	200	4,903	3,620	100	1,183
1933-34..........	5,736	100	5,836	---	---	---

Production -- South Manchurian Railway and Associated Manchurian Crop Estimates
Commission. Carryover -- Information from American Consular Reports. Exports-
American Consular Reports and Chinese Maritime Customs Returns.

The current demand from other sources for beans varies considerably.
South China will increase no doubt her imports compared with the previous
year since the Kwangtung Provincial Foodstuffs Commission has permitted the
importation of limited quantities of Manchurian beans. Japan is not expected
to increase her bean imports. The demand from the East Indies is not expected to improve due to accumulation of domestic vegetable oils.

The demand for beancake during 1933-34 is not expected to improve
substantially. In Japan low prices of agricultural products and cheap commer-
cial fertilizers will no doubt prevent increased takings. America will
probably not take larger quantities of beancake meal due to price advances in
United States currency. China may take a somewhat larger quantity but imports
are not expected to equal the quantity imported during the 1931-32 season.
Formosa during the past year has taken an increased interest in Manchurian
bean cake and may take a larger quantity this season.

South China boycott restrictions have been relaxed and takings of
bean oil during the 1933-34 year may be somewhat larger than last year. The
demand from other sources is not expected to show much change.

Soy bean prices in local currency at the Dairen exchange have been
on a downward trend since July 1929 and are now the lowest since 1921. Prices
during the past six weeks have declined very rapidly due to the small volume
of European buying. Bean oil and bean cake prices have in general followed
bean prices. The prices for bean cake have fallen to a greater extent than
beans and bean oil.

MANCHURIAN SOYBEAN OUTPUT LARGER THAN LAST YEAR, CONT'D

MANCHURIA: Total exports of soy beans and bean products,
1927-28 to 1932-33

Year ended September 30	Soy beans	Soy-bean cake and meal	Soy-bean oil	Total exports
	Short tons	Short tons	Short tons	Short tons
1927-28 a/........	2,534,000	1,822,000	136,000	4,492,000
1928-29 a/..	2,948,000	1,578,000	131,000	4,657,000
1929-30 a/.....	2,526,000	1,725,000	163,000	4,414,000
1930-31 a/........... ..	2,449,000	1,900,000	170,000	4,569,000
1931-32 b/...	3,014,859	1,545,471	156,648	4,716,978
1932-33 b/...............	2,491,681	1,054,965	73,379	3,620,025

China Maritime Customs Quarterly Trade Returns, and for the past year from
South Manchuria Railway Report. a/ Exports from Harbin, Dairen, Newchwang,
Antung, Lungchintsun and Hunchun. b/ Exports from Harbin, Dairen, Newchwang
and Antung. Lungchintsun, Hunchun and Manchouli not included.

At the beginning of the crop year October 1 the disposal of the large
bean crop was considered a very serious problem. Many trade authorities were
estimating a million tons of beans in excess of the demand for the crop year.
However, with the continual decline in prices at Dairen, European buyers made
heavy purchases in October and November. During December cargo space for shipments to Europe was not sufficient for the demand in spite of the fact that
ocean rates were recently advanced two shillings per short ton. During the
first three months of the current crop year bean exports to Europe have exceeded those of a year ago. In December and early January there was a sharp decline
in European buying but with present low prices it is believed that Europe will
resume buying and may set a record volume of bean imports for the crop year.

Review of 1932-33 crop year

The total bean exports from Manchuria during 1932-33 were 23 percent
below the previous year and the smallest quantity since 1925-26. Total exports
to China decreased 78 percent compared with the 1931-32 crop year. However,
according to available information Manchuria exported to Europe during the
1932-33 crop year the largest quantity of beans on record. The total amount of
beans exported to Europe during the year equaled 61,766,000 bushels in addition
to the equivalent of 3,350,000 bushels of beans in the form of bean cake and
bean oil. Prices for beans during the crop year were slightly lower than the
previous year but were fairly steady until August when reports of the large new
crop weakened the market.

The 1932 Manchurian soy bean crop was the smallest since 1926. The
South Manchurian Railway estimated the 1932 production at 4,703,000 short tons
which figure appears to have been somewhat too high. The planted acreage was
below the previous year and the excessive rainfall during the summer considerably reduced the yield especially in North Manchuria. The quality of the beans
was inferior to the crop of the previous season.

MANCHURIAN SOYBEAN OUTPUT LARGER THAN LAST YEAR, CONT'D

The bean exports for the 1932-33 crop year were 20 percent below the previous year. Japan, China and the East Indies took smaller amounts while the European countries increased their purchases compared with the 1931-32 crop year. China took 82 percent less Manchurian beans than the previous year due in considerable degree to the boycott. For the 1932-33 season bean shipments to Europe represented 74 percent of the total beans exported. Europe evidently has been finding it profitable to crush soy beans since she has been decreasing imports of Manchurian bean oil and bean cake and increasing imports of beans. During the World War Europe bought large quantities of bean oil heavily since freight rates were high and industrial plants found other work more profitable.

MANCHURIA: Exports of soy beans and products by countries of destination, 1931-32 and 1932-33

Product and crop year October – September	Europe	Lenin-grad	Japan a/	China	East Indies	United States	Others	Total
	Short tons	Short tons	Short tons	Short tons	Short tons	Short tons	Short tons	Short tons
Beans –								
1931-32	1,544,206	202,665	546,344	641,163	79,797	199	485	3,014,859
1932-33	1,853,410	0	461,065	116,498	60,222	77	409	2,491,681
Bean cake –								
1931-32	71,491		998,978	442,534		255	15,114	17,099	1,545,471
1932-33	62,983		770,878	177,871		132	40,990	2,111	1,054,965
Bean oil –								
1931-32.	46,805		375	107,832 b/		1,063	573	156,648
1932-33	37,356		179	33,504		2,025	315	73,379

Dairen American Consular Reports. a/ Includes exports to Korea and Formosa.
b/ Exports of 7,934 short tons from Newchwang during June were to China and the South Seas.

The total bean cake exports from Manchuria for the 1932-33 crop year were 32 percent below the 1931-32 crop year. Japan took a smaller amount but a larger percent of the total volume exported during the 1932-33 season. America took nearly three times the amount compared with the previous year. The price of Manchuria bean meal at Dairen of 50 to 60 cents United States currency per hundredweight attracted Pacific Coast buyers. China took 60 percent less bean cake compared with the Previous crop year. Up to the 1932-33 season, China had been increasing her imports of bean cake. For a number of years, Europe has been decreasing her purchases of bean cake.

The bean oil exports from Manchuria during the 1932-33 crop year were the smallest since 1915. Europe and China are practically the only markets for bean oil. European purchases have continued to decline for several years.

MANCHURIAN SOYBEAN OUTPUT LARGER THAN LAST YEAR, CONT'D

The 1932 Chinese boycott of Manchurian goods interrupted the upward trend
of imports of bean oil into China. The bean crushing industry in Manchuria
has been affected severly in the past year because of the poor demand for
bean oil and bean cake. During November 1931 thirty two Dairen bean mills
operated at 55 percent capacity and in November 1932, twenty two mills operated
at 31 percent capacity. November is considered one of the peak months of
activity.

MANCHURIA: Average monthly price of soy beans and soy bean products at
Dairen, in silver yen and United States currency and price
of crude soy-bean oil at New York, 1931-32 to 1933-34

Year and month	Beans		Bean cake		Bean oil		Soy-bean oil at New York
	Silver ¥ per picul a/	U.S.cents per pound	Silver ¥ per cake of 61 lbs	U.S.cents per pound	Silver ¥ per picul	U.S.cents per pound	U.S. cents per pound
1931-32							
Oct.	5.38	.96	1.77	.69	14.24	2.53	5.3
Nov.	5.26	.95	1.72	.68	13.53	2.45	5.1
Dec.	4.84	.90	1.71	.69	11.88	2.19	4.7
Jan.	5.06	.85	1.74	.66	12.80	2.15	4.5
Feb.	5.12	.99	1.76	.74	13.00	2.53	4.3
Mar.	4.78	.84	1.65	.63	12.70	2.23	4.3
Apr.	4.81	.86	1.60	.60	12.95	2.21	4.3
May	5.23	.86	1.72	.61	13.82	2.26	4.3
June	5.26	.87	1.63	.58	13.80	2.26	4.1
July	5.25	.85	1.60	.57	14.20	2.30	4.1
Aug.	5.67	.97	1.66	.62	15.52	2.65	4.1
Sept.	5.52	.95	1.72	.65	15.73	2.72	4.1
1932-33							
Oct.	5.14	.86	1.61	.59	13.45	2.25	4.3
Nov.	5.10	.84	1.65	.59	13.97	2.30	4.2
Dec.	5.23	.79	1.73	.57	14.30	2.17	4.1
Jan.	5.19	.79	1.72	.57	14.46	2.37	4.2
Feb.	4.88	.75	1.58	.54	13.89	2.13	4.3
Mar.	4.86	.76	1.50	.50	13.70	2.15	4.5
Apr.	4.82	.78	1.51	.54	13.69	2.22	4.7
May	4.89	.85	1.52	.58	13.80	2.40	6.1
June	5.11	.95	1.63	.66	14.09	2.63	6.9
July	4.98	1.05	1.53	.71	14.76	3.12	8.9
Aug.	4.44	.90	1.37	.61	13.50	2.74	8.2
Sept.	4.31	.92	1.29	.60	12.57	2.67	8.0
1933-34							
Oct.	4.09	.87	1.21	.56	11.16	2.38	7.4
Nov.	3.92	.93	1.22	.63	11.07	2.63	7.1
Dec.	3.63	.88	1.16	.61	9.77	2.35	6.8
Jan.	3.28	.80	1.06	.56	8.76	2.14	6.6

"Finance and Commerce" (a Shanghai weekly trade journal) and the United States
Department of Labor, Bureau of Labor Statistics, Monthly Bulletins. a/ One
picul is equivalent to 133-1/3 pounds.

UNITED STATES: Exports of principal agricultural products,
July-January, 1932-33 and 1933-34

Article exported	Unit	July - January			
		Quantity		Value	
		1932-33	1933-34	1932-33	1933-34
ANIMALS AND ANIMAL PRODUCTS:		Thousands	Thousands	1,000 dollars	1,000 dollars
LIVE ANIMALS:					
Cattle	No.	2	2	98	132
Hogs	No.	17	3	146	46
Sheep and goats	No.	1 a/		4	7
Poultry, live	Lb.	28	25	15	18
DAIRY PRODUCTS:					
Butter	Lb.	934	794	217	183
Cheese	Lb.	783	732	134	141
Milk-					
Fresh & sterilized	Gal.	17	25	16	18
Condensed	Lb.	3,969	2,319	519	271
Dried	Lb.	1,740	1,504	345	317
Evaporated	Lb.	19,584	18,702	1,131	1,166
Infants' foods, malted	Lb.	814	934	213	269
Eggs in the shell	Doz.	999	1,116	249	243
MEATS AND MEAT PRODUCTS:					
Beef and veal, fresh	Lb.	1,015	2,033	171	253
Beef, pickled or cured	Lb.	5,506	8,223	357	470
Beef, canned	Lb.	583	686	128	186
Total beef	Lb.	7,104	10,942	656	909
Pork-					
Carcasses, fresh	Lb.	81	1,266	4	111
Loins and other fresh	Lb.	4,488	12,836	369	1,364
Total fresh pork	Lb.	4,569	14,102	373	1,475
Bacon	Lb.	11,041	14,550	755	1,150
Canned	Lb.	4,872	6,495	961	1,683
Hams and shoulders	Lb.	37,910	43,885	3,758	5,343
Pickled or salted	Lb.	8,777	10,841	554	707
Sides,Cumberland & Wiltshire	Lb.	484	555	36	62
Total pork	Lb.	67,653	90,428	6,437	10,420
Mutton and lamb	Lb.	131	258	21	38
Poultry and game, fresh	Lb.	646	969	135	179
Other canned meats, incl.					
canned poultry	Lb.	387	312	60	55
Sausage, canned	Lb.	414	637	85	139
Sausage, not canned	Lb.	1,342	1,612	233	297
Sausage casings	Lb.	15,376	21,631	1,730	4,368
Other meats, including meat					
extracts and edible offal	Lb.	15,276	22,191	1,074	1,750
Total meats	Lb.	108,329	148,980	10,431	18,155

Continued .

UNITED STATES: Exports of principal agricultural products,
July-January, 1932-33 and 1933-34, cont'd

Article exported	Unit	July - January			
		Quantity		Value	
		1932-33	1933-34	1932-33	1933-34
ANIMAL AND ANIMAL PRODUCTS CONT'D		Thousands	Thousands	1,000 dollars	1,000 dollars
OILS AND FATS, ANIMAL:					
Lard...................	Lb.	332,145	324,071	19,030	19,910
Lard, neutral..........	Lb.	3,666	2,708	234	186
Oleo oil...............	Lb.	24,701	17,102	1,343	1,012
Oleo stock.............	Lb.	3,964	6,744	215	387
Stearins and fatty acids...	Lb.	6,177	5,573	309	316
Tallow.................	Lb.	2,275	5,990	105	273
Other animal oils, greeses and fats............	Lb.	36,359	57,106	1,216	2,292
Total oils and fats......	Lb.	409,287	419,294	22,452	24,376
VEGETABLE PRODUCTS:					
Coffee.................	Lb.	2,405	6,188	426	1,061
Cotton....(500 lbs.).......	Bale	5,808	5,929	212,060	296,786
Cotton linters (500 lbs.)..	Bale	116	128	1,258	2,212
FRUITS:					
Apples-					
Fresh...............	Bskt	234	390	356	608
Fresh...............	Box	6,276	5,577	7,305	6,967
Fresh...............	Bbl.	1,353	890	5,425	3,467
Dried...............	Lb.	25,054	30,025	1,547	2,532
Apricots, dried...........	Lb.	27,779	30,988	1,954	3,140
Grapefruit.............	Box	365	414	933	1,036
Oranges...............	Box	1,620	1,636	3,592	3,577
Pears, fresh...........	Lb.	114,435	100,410	3,961	3,614
Prunes, dried..........	Lb.	130,415	140,220	4,882	7,503
Raisins...............	Lb.	91,547	71,060	4,072	3,229
Canned fruit...........	Lb.	178,978	224,407	11,276	14,599
GRAINS, FLOUR AND MEAL:					
Barley, excluding flour...	Bu.	6,344	3,865	2,369	2,202
Buckwheat, excluding flour.	Bu.	33	9	17	5
Corn, including cornmeal..	Bu.	6,476	3,646	2,274	2,131
Malt..................	Bu.	141	90	116	95
Oats, including oatmeal....	Bu.	3,982	986	1,340	946
Rice, including flour, meal and broken rice....	Lb.	117,631	61,392	2,039	2,035
Rye, excluding flour.......	Bu.	286	16	136	11
Wheat.................	Bu.	19,478	7,649	11,026	4,758
Wheat, flour...........	Bbl.	2,654	2,332	8,235	9,039
Wheat, including flour.	Bu.	31,950	18,608	19,261	13,797

Continued

UNITED STATES: Exports of principal agricultural products,
July-January, 1932-33 and 1933-34, cont'd.

Article exported	Unit	July - January			
		Quantity		Value	
		1932-33	1933-34	1932-33	1933-34
VEGETABLE PRODUCTS, CONT'D:		Thousands	Thousands	1,000 dollars	1,000 dollars
OILSEED PRODUCTS:					
Cottonseed cake and meal	L.Ton	100	60	1,803	1,392
Linseed cake and meal...	"	61	164	1,749	5,034
Cottonseed, oil, crude..	Lb.	22,235	11,263	657	389
Cottonseed oil, refined.	Lb.	5,694	4,510	340	291
Sugar (2,000 lb.).........	Ton	23	34	706	1,133
TOBACCO LEAF:					
Bright flue-cured.......	Lb.	187,243	215,001	34,775	55,226
Burley..................	Lb.	5,506	6,436	536	815
Dark-fired Ky.& Tennessee	Lb.	30,775	43,206	3,218	3,717
Dark Virginia...........	Lb.	8,110	7,025	1,569	1,116
Maryland and Ohio export	Lb.	7,577	6,761	1,599	1,555
Green River (Pryor).....	Lb.	982	725	113	69
One-sucker leaf.........	Lb.	496	731	59	55
Cigar leaf..............	Lb.	220	1,364	89	397
Black fat, water baler and dark African......	Lb.	5,107	5,435	774	772
Preique.................	Lb.	33	31	13	11
Total leaf tobacco...	Lb.	246,049	286,715	42,745	63,733
Stems, trimmings, scrap.	Lb.	13,918	10,815	594	533
VEGETABLES:					
Beans, dried............	Lb.	6,034	5,176	192	232
Peas, dried.............	Lb.	1,748	1,363	83	76
Onions..................	Lb.	24,107	15,791	237	207
Potatoes, white.........	Lb.	40,897	25,234	373	444
Vegetables, canned......	Lb.	12,929	18,434	1,064	1,563
MISC. VEGETABLE PRODUCTS:					
Drugs, herbs,roots, etc.	Lb.	2,655	3,079	838	1,109
Glucose.................	Lb.	23,856	31,978	565	805
Hops....................	Lb.	2,046	6,724	511	2,351
Starch, corn...........	Lb.	32,136	44,105	804	1,201
GRAND TOTAL				375,830	497,388

Foreign Agricultural Service,   Compiled from official records of the Bureau of
Foreign and Domestic Commerce.
a/ Less than 500.

UNITED STATES: Imports[a/] of principal agricultural products,
July-January, 1932-33 and 1933-34

Article imported	Unit	July-January			
		Quantity		Value	
		1932-33	1933-34	1932-33	1933-34
ANIMALS AND ANIMAL PRODUCTS:		Thousands	Thousands	1,000 dollars	1,000 dollars
LIVE ANIMALS:					
Cattle	No.	48	32	818	581
Hogs	Lb.	18	2	1	b/
Horses	No.	1	1	204	328
Sheep, lambs and goats	No.	b/	2	2	8
DAIRY PRODUCTS:					
Butter	Lb.	430	411	86	72
Casein	Lb.	598	7,611	18	426
Cheese-					
Swiss	Lb.	6,840	4,715	1,525	1,196
Other	Lb.	26,367	20,719	5,923	4,742
Total cheese	Lb.	33,207	25,434	7,448	5,938
Cream	Gal.	51	25	71	31
Milk-					
Condensed and evaporated	Lb.	505	466	23	22
Dried and malted	Lb.	299	336	64	50
Whole, skimmed & buttermilk	Gal.	13	33	2	6
EGGS AND EGG PRODUCTS:					
Eggs in the shell	Doz.	163	128	21	21
Eggs, whole, dried	Lb.	3	1	1	b/
Eggs, whole, frozen	Lb.	b/	110	b/	9
Egg albumen, dried	Lb.	1,187	178	492	76
Egg albumen, frozen	Lb.	0	0	0	0
Yolks, dried	Lb.	1,214	1,995	128	138
Yolks, frozen	Lb.	293	235	25	17
Hides and skins	Lb.	98,588	230,950	10,888	35,120
MEATS AND MEAT PRODUCTS:					
Beef and veal, fresh	Lb.	511	115	42	12
Beef & veal,pickled or cured	Lb.	511	346	35	20
Mutton and lamb, fresh	Lb.	35	2	3	b/
Pork-,					
Fresh	Lb.	1,005	174	91	22
Hams,shoulders and bacon..	Lb.	1,513	777	305	214
Pickled, salted and other	Lb.	533	369	157	131
Sausage casings	Lb.	6,942	8,450	2,218	3,939
Silk, raw	Lb.	47,541	39,938	63,601	68,445
Wool, unmanufactured	Lb.	23,084	154,210	2,031	19,934

Continued

UNITED STATES: Imports[a]/of principal agricultural products,
July-January, 1932-33 and 1933-34, cont'd.

Article imported	Unit	July - January			
		Quantity		Value	
		1932-33	1933-34	1932-33	1933-34
		Thousands	Thousands	1,000 dollars	1,000 dollars
VEGETABLE PRODUCTS:					
Cacao beans	Lb.	273,598	257,854	10,704	11,145
Coffee	Lb.	761,443	914,375	71,447	66,589
Cotton (478 lbs.)	Bale	.71	85	3,161	5,039
FEED AND FODDER:					
Beet pulp, dried	L. Ton	.10	5	139	77
Bran, shorts, etc.-					
Of direct importation	L. Ton	10	81	113	1,213
Withdrawn bonded mills ...	L. Ton	.26	87	294	1,070
Hay (2,000 lb.)	Ton	4	1	25	9
Oil cake and oil-cake meal-					
Bean (soy)	Lb.	16,174	41,829	135	406
Coconut	Lb.	6,177	18,747	45	114
Cottonseed	Lb.	315	2,262	3	13
Linseed	Lb.	8,660	12,259	62	106
All other	Lb.	413	3,255	3	28
Total	Lb.	31,739	78,352	248	667
FRUITS:					
Bananas	Bunch	27,430	22,107	13,216	11,177
Berries, natural state, etc.	Lb.	2,784	4,026	188	206
Currants	Lb.	5,850	5,292	279	319
Dates	Lb.	44,878	42,922	1,534	1,704
Figs	Lb.	6,025	5,994	367	404
Grapes	cu.ft.	12	9	22	24
Lemons	Lb.	5,620	2,362	160	68
Limes	Lb.	1,893	1,790	55	49
Pineapples-					
Fresh		c/	c/	124	51
Prepared or preserved, etc.	Lb.	1,985	2,022	95	97
Product of the Philippines	Lb.	3,696	19	208	b/
Raisins	Lb.	1,169	1,063	97	122
Olives-					
In brine	Gal.	2,210	3,038	815	1,596
Dried or ripe	Lb.	169	58	10	5
GRAINS AND GRAIN PRODUCTS:					
Corn	Bu.	138	109	55	55
Oats	Bu.	5	128	2	47
Rice-					
Uncleaned	Lb.	1,248	1,929	23	43
Cleaned (except patna) ...	Lb.	7,991	6,356	190	149
Patna	Lb.	396	590	12	19
Meal, flour and broken ...	Lb.	335	7,914	10	112
Wheat, including flour	Bu.	5,747	6,750	2,767	4,238

Continued

UNITED STATES: Imports of, principal agricultural products,
July-January, 1932-33 and 1933-34 cont'd.

a/

Article imported	Unit	July – January			
		Quantity		Value	
		1932-33	1933-34	1932-33	1933-34
		Thousands	Thousands	1,000 dollars	1,000 dollars
VEGETABLE PRODUCTS: CONT'D.					
Nuts.................................		c/	c/	5,501	6,340
OILS, VEGETABLE:					
Tung oil......................	Lb.	43,822	81,643	1,719	3,726
Cacao butter................	Lb.	9	3	2	1
Coconut, product of the P.I...	Lb.	135,238	208,777	3,884	5,449
Linseed oil...................	Lb.	17	11,363	1	412
Olive oil, edible...........	Lb.	36,819	35,049	3,346	3,727
Olive oil, inedible..........	Lb.	28,598	28,483	1,141	1,476
Palmkernel....................	Lb.	2,239	7,540	72	207
Palm oil......................	Lb.	144,220	176,421	3,523	4,620
Peanut oil....................	Lb.	648	764	37	53
Soybean oil...................	Lb.	1	3,669 b/		120
OILSEEDS:					
Castor beans.................	Lb.	38,863	86,406	707	1,503
Copra	Lb.	274,707	452,311	4,713	5,993
Flaxseed.....................	Bu.	2,828	11,104	1,813	12,039
Sesame seed..................	Lb.	16,018	26,117	312	536
Seeds, except oilseeds........		c/	c/	1,474	2,487
Spices...........................	Lb.	52,369	66,137	4,519	5,752
Sugar	S.ton	1,495	1,422	48,168	55,996
Tea	Lb.	62,260	61,935	6,643	10,063
Tobacco leaf, unmanufactured...	.	30,836	16,144	11,240	8,764
Tobacco stems, not cut, etc....	Lb.	1,235	1,157	45	45
VEGETABLES:					
Beans–					
Dried	Lb.	5,353	12,868	130	452
Green or unripe............	Lb.	3,974	2,929	122	80
Chickpeas or garbanzos, dried.	Lb.	6,711	7,094	253	245
Garlic.......................	Lb.	3,169	3,265	74	103
Onions.......................	Lb.	1,907	1,344	23	21
Peas, except cowpeas & chickpeas					
Dried	Lb.	3,532	7,243	97	247
Green......................	Lb.	4,260	3,035	202	155
Potatoes, white.............	Lb.	6,860	57,928	103	842
Tomatoes, fresh.............	Lb.	16,262	13,040	404	282
Turnips......................	Lb.	63,593	68,981	280	562
Vegetables, canned...........	Lb.	41,246	44,427	1,540	1,897
Drugs, herbs, roots, etc. ...		c/	c/	2,599	3,722

Continued

UNITED STATES: Imports a/ of principal agricultural products,
July-January, 1932-33 and 1933-34 cont'd.

Article imported	Unit	July - January			
		Quality		Value	
		1932-33	1933-34	1932-33	1933-34
VEGETABLE PRODUCTS, CONT'D		Thousands	Thousands	1,000 dollars	1,000 dollars
FIBERS, VEGETABLE:					
Flax, unmanufactured	L.Ton	1	2	158	837
Hemp, unmanufactured	L.Ton	b/	1	24	124
Jute & jute butts, unmfd.	L.Ton	15	35	795	2,262
Kapok	L.Ton	5	6	764	1,232
Manila	L.Ton	15	24	872	1,451
New Zealand fiber	L.Ton	b/	b/	5	.2
Sisal and henequen	L.Ton	116	74	5,643	4,686
Rubber, crude	Lb.	501,533	704,717	15,656	42,686
GRAND TOTAL				323,739	433,051

Foreign Agricultural Service. Compiled from official records of the Bureau of
Foreign and Domestic Commerce.
a/ Beginning January 1, 1934, imports for consumption.
b/ Less than 500.
c/ Reported in value only.

- - - - - - - -

FRESH PEACHES: Exports to Canada from the United States and
Canadian production, 1925-1933

Calendar year	U. S. exports to Canada	Canadian production	United States production
	1,000 bushels	1,000 bushels	1,000 bushels
1925	312	202	46,562
1926	276	238	69,865
1927	344	348	45,463
1928	415	606	68,369
1929	402	673	44,977
1930	249	757	54,199
1931	209	882	76,596
1932	69	904	42,443
1933	51	825	43,326

Compiled by the Foreign Agricultural Service from official sources.

WHEAT: Closing prices of May futures

Date	Chicago		Kansas City		Minneapolis		Winnipeg a/		Liverpool a/		Buenos Aires b/	
	1933	1934	1933	1934	1933	1934	1933	1934	1933	1934	1933	1934
	Cents	Cents	Cents	Cents	Cents	Cents	Cents	Cents	Cents	Cents	Cents	Cents
High c/	50	93	44	86	49	88	42	70	50	70	40	54
Low c/	46	84	39	77	42	80	39	65	47	64	36	51
Feb. 10	48	90	42	83	46	86	40	68	48	65	36	52
17	48	90	42	83	46	86	40	67	48	65	36	53
24	47	88	41	79	45	83	39	67	47	65	36	53
Mar. 3	49	88	43	80	46	84	40	69	47	67	36	53

a/ Conversions at noon buying rate of exchange. b/ Prices are of day previous to other prices. c/ January 1 to date.

WHEAT: Weighted average cash price at stated markets

Week ended	All classes and grades six markets		No. 2 Hard Winter Kansas City		No. 1 Dk.N.Spring Minneapolis		No. 2 Amber Durum Minneapolis		No. 2 Red Winter St. Louis		Western White Seattle a/	
	1933	1934	1933	1934	1933	1934	1933	1934	1933	1934	1933	1934
	Cents	Cents	Cents	Cents	Cents	Cents	Cents	Cents	Cents	Cents	Cents	Cents
High b/	50	93	45	87	52	92	55	114	50	93	47	78
Low b/	46	82	42	81	48	84	49	92	48	89	44	74
Feb. 10	48	93	43	87	50	92	50	111	49	92	45	76
17	48	92	44	85	51	91	51	109	50	92	45	75
24	48	88	44	84	51	89	50	109	49	90	45	74
Mar. 3	48	85	44	82	50	87	51	105	49	89	44	

a/ Weekly average of daily cash quotations, basis No. 1 sacked 30 days delivery.
b/ January 1 to date.

WHEAT AND FLOUR: Prices c.i.f. Shanghai
and Manila, March 2, 1934 with comparisons a/

Date 1934	Shanghai				Manila
	Canadian No. 3 Cents	Australian F.A.Q. Cents	Argentine Cents	Shang flour Cents c	Cents d
Jan. 12	----	---	---	74	---
19	69	62	59	74	---
26	69	69	57	71	2.81
Feb. 2	71	60	58	73	2.95
9	----	60	55	73	2.95
23 e/	69	61	55	73	2.76
Mar. 2	64	60	53	71	2.71

a/ Converted at current exchange rate. b/ Soft patents. Straights are 12 to 15 cents less per barrel. c/ Per bag of 49 pounds. d/ Per barrel of 196 pounds. e/ No Shanghai quotations received for preceding week due to Chinese New Year. Manila price unchanged.

WHEAT, INCLUDING FLOUR: Exports from the United States, by countries, January, 1933 and 1934, and July-January, 1932-33 and 1933-34.

Country to which exported	Wheat, incl. flour July-January		Wheat January		Wheat flour January	
	1932-33	1933-34	1933	1934	1933	1934
	1,000 bushels	1,000 bushels	1,000 bushels	1,000 bushels	1,000 barrels	1,000 barrels
Greece	3,152	15	274	0	0	a/
United Kingdom	1,852	305	27	64	6	7
Belgium	1,818	164	300	100	1	1
Netherlands	1,170	331	0	0	25	4
Irish Free State	1,002	736	0	345	6	5
France	974	20	4	20	a/	0
Italy	583	269	126	0	5	1
Norway	473	310	0	0	a/	12
Germany	317	50	0	0	1	2
Denmark	167	113	0	0	4	3
Finland	110	67	0	0	a/	1
Malta, Gozo, and Cyprus	56	71	0	0	a/	a/
Sweden	50	7	0	0	a/	a/
Other Europe	48	62	0	a/	1	a/
Total Europe	11,772	2,520	731	529	49	36
Canada	506	26	3	3	1	a/
Cuba	1,839	1,944	a/	1	54	67
Haiti, Republic of	432	377	a/	0	15	18
Panama	315	627	0	291	9	9
Mexico	28	38	a/	a/ 1	1	a/
Brazil	8,817	642	1,009	0	3	16
Peru	47	222	0	108	1	2
Colombia	23	13	0	0	a/	a/
Hong Kong	1,310	616	2	0	34	16
China	546	4,340	0	637	1	5
Kwantung	116	210	0	0	1	17
Japan	121	1,914	33	1,280	a/	a/
Philippine Islands	1,566	1,440	a/	0	40	69
Other Countries	4,512	3,679	15	18	115	107
Total exports	31,950	18,608	1,793	2,867	324	362
Total imports b/	5,747	6,750	800	864	a/	a/
Total reexports	454	a/ c/	0	---	0	---
Net exports	26,567	11,858	993	2,003	324	362

Foreign Agricultural Service. Compiled from official records of the Bureau of Foreign and Domestic Commerce.
a/ Less than 500.
b/ Imports for consumption beginning January 1, 1934.
c/ Six months, July - December.

PERU: Imports of wheat and flour, 1913-1932

Year	Wheat	Flour	Total wheat and flour a/
	Bushels	Barrels	Bushels
1913..............	1,884,000	27,079	2,005,856
1919..............	2,734,000	46,064	2,941,288
1920..............	1,947,000	74,793	2,283,568
1921..............	2,185,000	82,691	2,557,110
1922..............	2,146,000	128,152	2,722,684
1923..............	2,345,000	79,441	2,783,484
1924..............	3,521,000	75,663	3,861,484
1925..............	2,844,000	72,672	3,171,024
1926..............	2,714,000	82,779	3,086,506
1927..............	2,787,000	96,987	3,223,442
1928..............	2,772,000	96,815	3,207,668
1929..............	3,759,000	105,973	4,235,878
1930..............	2,501,000	87,119	2,893,036
1931..............	3,788,000	80,292	4,149,314
1932..............	3,044,000	40,837	3,227,766

Official sources. a/ Flour converted to wheat on basis of 4.5 bushels per bbl.

PERU: Imports of wheat and flour, by principal
countries of origin, 1928-1932

Country of origin	1928	1929	1930	1931	1932
WHEAT	Bushels	Bushels	Bushels	Bushels	Bushels
United States....	844,000	404,000	19,000	151,000	2,000
Australia........	1,043,000	1,640,000	522,000	1,103,000	1,257,000
Argentina........	384,000	1,483,000	790,000	1,829,000	1,253,000
Chile............	333,000	8,000	364,000	44,000	7,000
Canada...........	168,000	224,000	806,000	550,000	353,000
Others...........	—	—	—	111,000	172,000
Total.........	2,772,000	3,759,000	2,501,000	3,788,000	3,044,000
FLOUR	Barrels	Barrels	Barrels	Barrels	Barrels
United States....	96,391	104,844	71,618	74,715	33,182
Chile............	—	596	15,482	3,306	6,776
Argentina........	—	—	—	467	—
Canada...........	—	—	—	1,788	874
Others...........	424	533	19	16	5
Total.........	96,815	105,973	87,119	80,292	40,837

Official sources.

FEED GRAINS AND RYE: Weekly average price per bushel of corn, rye, oats and barley at loading markets a/

Week ended	Corn						Rye		Oats		Barley	
	Chicago				Buenos Aires		Minneapolis		Chicago		Minneapolis	
	No. 3 Yellow		Futures		Futures		No. 2		No. 3 White		Special No. 2	
	1933	1934	1933	1934	1933	1934	1933	1934	1933	1934	1933	1934
	Cents	Cents	Cents	Cents	Cents	Cents	Cents	Cents	Cents	Cents	Cents	Cents
High b/....:	24	50	28	53	30	42	33	64	16	37	27	73
Low b/....:	22	48	24	51	27	40	32	59	15	33	24	68
			May	May	Mar.	Mar.						
Feb. 3 ....:	24	50	26	53	30	41	32	64	15	36	25	72
					May	May						
10....:	24	49	26	52	27	40	32	62	15	37	26	71
17 ....:	23	49	26	52	27	41	32	61	15	36	27	72
24 ....:	23	48	25	51	27	42	33	59	15	35	25	71
Mar. 3 ....:	22	48	24	51	27	41	32	60	15	33	24	68

a/ Cash prices are weighted averages of reported sales; future prices are simple averages of daily quotations. b/ For period January 1 to latest date shown.

FEED GRAINS: Movement from principal exporting countries

Item	Exports for year		Shipments 1934, week ended a/			Exports as far as reported		
	1931-32	1932-33 b/	Feb. 17	Feb. 24	Mar. 3	July 1 to and incl. b/	1932-33 b/	1933-34 b/
	1,000 bushels	1,000 bushels	1,000 bushels	1,000 bushels	1,000 bushels		1,000 bushels	1,000 bushels
BARLEY,EXPORTS: c/								
United States....:	5,084	9,155	152	67	66:Mar.3		6,854	4,421
Canada..........:	14,505	6,750				:Jan.31	5,936	1,070
Argentina........:	13,822	17,431	d/1,263	d/1,084	d/1,346:Mar.3		6,763	12,251
Danube coun. d/..:	29,653	21,537	74	396	198:Mar.3		18,553	22,829
Total........:	63,064	54,873					38,106	40,571
OATS, EXPORTS: c/								
United States...:	4,437	5,361	1	0	0:Mar.3		4,304	989
Canada..........:	18,467	14,158				:Jan.31	9,864	4,282
Argentina........:	52,194	33,891	d/ 753:d/	434:d/	468:Mar.3		21,994	13,376
Danube coun. d/..:	947	892	0	0	0:Mar.3		690	1,589
Total.......:	76,045	54,302					36,852	20,236
CORN,EXPORTS: e/						f/		
United States...:	6,095	7,259	5	55	102:Mar.3		3,948	2,159
Danube coun. d/..:	38,374	73,311	128	230	459:Mar.3		31,495	4,963
Argentina........:	314,834	186,050	d/3,389	d/2,437	d/2,098:Mar.3		58,342	82,396
South Africa d/..:	16,071	11,409	0	0	0:Mar.3		8,293	0
Total.........:	375,374	278,029					102,078	89,518
United States imports........:	393	163				:Nov-Jan	65	Nov-Jan 62

Compiled from official and trade sources. a/ The weeks shown in these columns are nearest to the date shown. b/ Preliminary. c/ Year beginning July 1. d/ Trade sources. e/ Year beginning November 1. f/ November 1 to and including.

HOPS: Acreage and production in specified countries, 1931 to 1933

	Acreage			Production		
	1931	1932	1933 a/	1931	1932	1933
	Acres	Acres	Acres	1,000 pounds	1,000 pounds	1,000 pounds
North America:						
Canada b/.........	925	690	---	1,230	790	---
United States c/..	21,400	22,000	26,500	26,410	24,058	36,440
Europe:						
England and Wales..	d/19,528	d/16,531	d/16,895	18,928	21,056	24,19
Belgium............	2,051	1,000	2,000	1,149	1,531	1,76
France......	5,893	4,361	4,581	1,178	1,711	3,64
Germany............	25,325	19,800	23,638	17,152	10,928	14,97
Austria.......	126	111	---+	44	---	---
Czechoslovakia.....	30,194	24,353	26,571	27,177	16,583	12,91
Hungary............	566	243	358	274	141	---
Yugoslavia....:....	e/ 5,683	e/ 4,447	e/ 4,408	e/ 3,636	e/ 3,085	---
Rumania............	210	72	---	107	33	---
Poland.............	e/ 6,177	5,000	9,000	e/ 3,967	3,436	---
Total Eur.Co's. reporting acreage and production, all years......	82,991	66,045	73,685	65,584	51,809	57,49
Oceania:						
Australia.....	1,036	---	---	1,810		
New Zealand.... ...	466	e/ 650	---	e/ 600	e/ 840	
Total co's. report acreage and production all years	104,391	88,045	100,185	91,994	75,867	93,9
Estimated world total, excluding Russia f/......	119,580	100,000	117,000	103,662	86,000	104,0

Bureau of Agricultural Economics. Official sources and International Institute of Agriculture except as otherwise stated.

a/   Preliminary.
b/   British Columbia.
c/   Principal producing states.
d/   These figures include the acreage left unpicked which was estimated at 1,60 acres in 1931, 200 acres in 1932, and 20 acres in 1933.
e/   Unofficial estimate.
f/   Exclusive of acreage and production in minor producing countries for which no data are available.

COTTON, UNMANUFACTURED: Exports from the United States, by countries,
January and August-January 1932-33 and 1933-34.

(Bales of 500 lbs. gross)

Country to which exported	August - January		January	
	1932-33	1933-34	1933	1934
	Bales	Bales	Bales	Bales
LONG AND SHORT STAPLE:				
Germany	1,166,184	970,633	162,553	165,450
United Kingdom	918,457	891,690	151,917	128,421
France	625,739	620,688	79,662	90,488
Italy	481,169	452,961	86,178	58,764
Spain	192,546	184,960	32,045	34,456
Belgium	132,921	87,537	18,317	15,201
Poland and Danzig	96,116	154,974	19,104	25,191
Netherlands	80,759	75,836	12,014	8,589
Sweden	42,482	50,315	6,113	7,793
Portugal	38,562	35,539	8,261	6,920
Soviet Russia (Europe)	0	21,774	0	0
Other Europe	50,572	76,377	7,079	28,378
Total Europe	3,815,507	3,623,284	583,243	569,651
Canada	102,439	123,677	15,915	896
Japan	1,167,151	1,244,670	180,517	174,828
China	170,699	167,585	40,598	24,577
British India	41,069	17,713	14,776	819
Other countries	56,758	29,420	1,691	10,852
Total exports	5,333,623	5,206,349	836,740	781,623
Total imports a/ b/	61,994	72,574	22,334	13,324
Total reexports	5,495	c/ 7,251	16	---
Net exports	5,275,114	5,141,006	814,422	768,299
LINTERS:				
Germany	31,831	36,889	7,671	8,779
United Kingdom	19,483	26,860	1,902	2,358
France	18,693	12,116	2,223	4,797
Netherlands	10,405	6,333	1,912	1,755
Belgium	7,100	1,827	108	265
Other Europe	2,449	2,487	193	233
Total Europe	89,961	86,512	14,009	18,187
Canada	6,597	5,537	1,545	690
Japan	6,988	9,519	378	2,027
Other Countries	964	3,821	224	1,553
Total Exports	104,510	105,379	16,156	22,457

Foreign Agricultural Service . Compiled from official records of the Bureau of
Foreign and Domestic Commerce.
a/ Bales of 478 lbs. net.
b/ Imports for consumption beginning Jan. 1, 1934.
c/ Five months, August-December.

GRAINS: Exports from the United States, July 1 - Mar. 3, 1932-33 and 1933-34
PORK : Exports from the United States, Jan. 1 - Feb. 24,1933 and 1934

Commodity	July 1 - Mar.3:		Week ended			
	1932-33	1933-34	Feb.10	Feb. 17	Feb. 24	Mar. 3
GRAINS:	1,000 bushels	1,000 bushels	1,000 bushels	1,000 bushels	1,000 bushels	1,000 bushels
Wheat a/............:	20,424	10,991	1,384	85	863	963
Wheat flour b/......:	14,236	12,173	244	169	207	329
Rye................:	287	16	--	--	--	--
Corn ....:	6,747	3,603	94	5	55	102
Oats...............:	3,538	391	1	1	--	--
Barley a/..........:	6,854	4,421	232	152	67	66
	Jan. 1 - Feb.24					
	1933	1934				
	1,000 pounds	1,000 pounds	1,000 pounds	1,000 pounds	1,000 pounds	1,000 pounds
PORK:						
Hams and shoulders..:	5,782	4,763	244	434	641	c/
Bacon incl. sides...:	2,984	3,955	326	662	932	c/
Lard...............:	125,019	75,817	7,042	5,763	4,134	c/
Pickled pork.......:	1,818	1,644	193	166	223	c/

Division of Statistical and Historical Research. Source: Official records - Bureau of Foreign and Domestic Commerce. a/ Included this week: Pacific Ports wheat 959,000 bushels, flour 43,300 barrels, from San Francisco; barley 66,000 bushels, rice 5,650,000 pounds. b/ Includes flour milled in bond from Canadian wheat in terms of wheat. c/ Not available.

Wheat, including flour: Shipments from principal exporting countries as given by current trade sources, 1931-32 to 1933-34

Country	Total shipments		Shipments, 1934: weeks ended		Shipments July 1 - Mar. 3	
	1931-32	1932-33	Feb. 17	Feb.14 Mar. 3	1932-33	1933-34
	1,000 bushels	1,000 bushels	1,000 bushels	1,000 bushels 1,000 bushels	1,000 bushels	1,000 bushels
North America a/......:	333,638	298,504	3,696	4,239 4,014,220	876,152	989
Canada, 4 markets b/..:	206,258	289,257	631	1,822 1,673,203	710,131	773
United States c/......:	135,797	41,211	254	1,070 1,293	34,660	23,164
Argentina...........:	144,576	115,412	4,092	4,020 2,628	56,272	83,340
Australia...........:	161,288	153,400	1,986	2,588 1,352,100,976	63,766	
Russia d/...........:	71,664	17,408	400	0 0 16,840	25,536	
Danube and Bulgaria d/:	39,280	1,704	24	224 24 1,616	10,712	
British India.......:	c/2,913	c/ 871	0	0 0 0	0	0
Total e/ ....:	753,359	587,299	10,198	11,071 8,018,396,480	336,343	
Total European shipments a/ ....:	597,976	448,672	8,648	290,784	262,008	
Total ex-European shipments a/........:	194,464	164,256	1,920	90,568	75,872	

Division of Statistical and Historical Research. Compiled from official and trade sources. a/ Broomhall's Corn Trade News. b/ Fort William, Port Arthur, Vancouver, Prince Rupert, and New Westminster. c/ Official. d/ Black Sea shipments only. e/ Total of trade figures includes North America as reported by Broomhall's. f/ To February 17.

EXCHANGE RATES: Average daily, weekly and monthly values in New York
of specified currencies, December-March, 1933-34 a/

Country	Monetary unit	Mint par	1933 Month: Dec.	1934 Month Jan.	Month Feb.	Week ended Feb.17	Week ended Feb.24	Week ended Mar. 3	Daily Mar. 5
		Cents	Cents	Cents	Cents	Cents	Cents	Cents	Cents
Argentina ...:	Paper peso:	42.45	33.33:	33.50:	33.55:	33.72:	33.91:	33.80:	33.79
Canada ......:	Dollar ...:	100.00	100.55:	99.52:	99.17:	99.10:	99.28:	99.35:	99.39
China ....:	Shang.yuan:	b/	33.45:	34.00:	34.31:	34.70:	34.99:	34.79:	34.83
Denmark .....:	Krone ....:	26.80	22.85:	22.55:	22.47:	22.58:	22.70:	22.66:	22.66
England .....:	Pound ....:	486.66	511.59:	504.93:	503.26:	505.85:	508.61:	507.39:	506.93
France ......:	Franc ....:	3.92	6.12:	6.21:	6.46:	6.53:	6.54:	6.57:	6.58
Germany .....:	Reichsmark:	23.82	37.32:	37.59:	38.88:	39.11:	39.40:	39.57:	39.64
Italy ....:	Lira .....:	5.26	8.22:	8.51:	8.58:	8.69:	8.64:	8.58:	8.59
Japan ....:	Yen ......:	49.85	30.74:	30.11:	29.75:	29.91:	29.96:	29.89:	29.88
Mexico ......:	Peso .....:	49.85	27.74:	27.74:	27.73:	27.72:	27.75:	27.72:	27.73
Netherlands :	Guilder ..:	40.20	62.85:	63.62:	66.04:	66.67:	66.82:	67.13:	67.21
Norway ......:	Krone ....:	26.80	25.71:	25.37:	25.28:	25.41:	25.55:	25.49:	25.48
Spain ....:	Peseta ...:	19.30	12.79:	13.00:	13.30:	13.12:	13.42:	13.45:	13.54: 13.59
Sweden ......:	Krona ....:	26.80	26.39:	26.04:	25.96:	26.09:	26.23:	26.17:	26.15

Federal Reserve Board. a/ Noon buying rates for cable transfers. b/ Par varies
with the price of silver in New York.

EUROPEAN LIVESTOCK AND MEAT MARKETS
(By weekly cable)

Market and item	Unit	Week ended Mar. 1, 1933 a/	Week ended Feb. 22, 1934 a/	Week ended Mar. 1, 1934 a/
GERMANY:				
Receipts of hogs, 14 markets	Number	68,695	---	---
Prices of hogs, Berlin ....:	$ per 100 lbs.:	7.40	14.75	13.64
Prices of lard, tcs. Hamburg	"	5.90	13.47	13.57
UNITED KINGDOM b/:				
Arrivals of continental bacon :	Bales	73,581	50,290	48,446
Prices at Liverpool 1st. qual.:				
American green bellies .....:	$ per 100 lbs.:	6.88	Nominal	Nominal
Danish green sides ....:	"	9.73	22.04	21.71
Canadian green sides ......:	"	8.76	19.66	19.44
American short green hams ..:	"	8.55	22.73	22.48
American refined lard ......:	"	8.83	7.25	7.31

Liverpool quotations are on the basis of sales from importer-to-wholesalers.
a/ Converted at current rate of exchange. b/ Week ended Friday.

Index

	Page		Page
Late cables	276	Meat (pork):	
Crop and Market Prospects..	277	Exports, United States by	
- - - -		weeks, 1934............	306
AGRICULTURAL EXPORTS,UNITED		Prices, foreign markets,1934	307
STATES:		Rye, prices, U. S. March 3,1934	303
INDEX NUMBERS, JAN.1934	284	Peaches:	
Principal products, Jan.		Damage by cold, Canada,1934	284
1934..................	293	Exports to Canada, United	
Agricultural imports, prin-		States, 1925-1933.........	299
cipal products, U.S. Jan.		Production, 1925-1933:	
1934	296	Canada....................	299
Apples, production, Austra-		United States.............	299
lia and New Zealand,1934.	283	SOY BEANS, SITUATION, MANCHURIA,	
Cotton:		1933-34	288
Consumption, World, Aug.		Sugar, market control scheme,	
1933-Jan.1934.........	281	Great Britain, 1934........	286
Exports, U. S. Jan. 1934	305	Wheat:	
Yarn production, Japan,		Export certificate system,	
Jan. 1934.............	282	Germany, 1934............	277
Exchange rates, foreign,		Exports, U.S. January 1934..	301
March 5, 1934..........	307	Exports and imports, Germany	
Grains:		Aug.-Dec. 1931-1933	277
Exports, U. S. by weeks,		Prices, principal markets,	
1934.................	306	March 3, 1934............	300
Movement (feed), princi-		Production aid, Peru, 1934	278,302
pal countries, March 3		Shipments, principal coun-	
1934.................	303	tries, March 3, 1934......	306
Prices (feed), principal		Trade control and price fix-	
markets, March 3, 1934	303	ing, Chile, 1934.........	280
Hops, area and production		World sales, U. K. March 9,	
World, 1931-1933	284,304	1934	276